STECK-VAUGHN

PORTRAIT OF AMERICA

Texas

Steck-Vaughn Company
    Executive Editor   Diane Sharpe
    Senior Editor   Martin S. Saiewitz
    Design Manager   Pamela Heaney
    Photo Editor   Margie Foster

Proof Positive/Farrowlyne Associates, Inc.
Program Editorial, Revision Development, Design, and Production

Consultant: Jean Carefoot, Archivist, State Archives Division, Texas State Library

Published by Raintree Steck-Vaughn Publishers, an imprint of Steck-Vaughn Company.

A Turner Educational Services, Inc. book. Based on the Portrait of America television series by R. E. (Ted) Turner.

Library of Congress Cataloging-in-Publication Data

Thompson, Kathleen.
    Texas / Kathleen Thompson.
       p.   cm. — (Portrait of America)
    "Based on the Portrait of America television series"—T.p. verso.
    "A Turner book."
    Includes index.
    ISBN 0-8114-7389-9 (library binding).—ISBN 0-8114-7470-4 (softcover)
    1. Texas—Juvenile literature. I. Portrait of America
(Television program) II. Title. III. Series: Thompson, Kathleen.
Portrait of America.
F386.3.T46 1996
976.4—dc20
                               95-30264
                                   CIP
                                   AC

Acknowledgments
The publishers wish to thank the following for permission to reproduce photographs:
Pp. 7 & 8 Texas Highways Magazine; p. 10 (top) Institute For Texan Cultures, (bottom) Texas Highways Magazine; p. 12 North Wind Picture Archives; p. 13 (top) Institute For Texan Cultures, (bottom) Texas Highways Magazine; p. 14 Institute For Texan Cultures; p. 15 Texas State Library; pp. 17 & 18 Texas Highways Magazine; p. 19 Texas State Library; p. 20 John F. Kennedy Library; pp. 21–23 Texas Highways Magazine; p. 24 Professional Rodeo Cowboys Association; p. 25 Texas Highways Magazine; pp. 26 & 27 Texas State Library; pp. 28, 30, 31 Texas Highways Magazine; pp. 32 & 33 H & H Foods; p. 34 © Bob Daemmrich; pp. 36 & 37 Texas Highways Magazine; p. 38 (top) Texas Highways Magazine; p. 39 Texas Highways Magazine; p. 40 The Institute For Texan Cultures, The San Antonio Light Collection; pp. 41, 42, 44 Texas Highways Magazine; p. 46 One Mile Up; p. 47 (top left) One Mile Up, (top right, bottom) Texas Highways Magazine.

STECK-VAUGHN

PORTRAIT OF AMERICA

Texas

Kathleen Thompson

A Turner Book

RSVP

RAINTREE
STECK-VAUGHN
PUBLISHERS

The Steck-Vaughn Company

Austin, Texas

Texas

Amarillo

Quanah

Lubbock

Red River

Dallas

Abilene

Fort Worth

GUADALUPE MOUNTAINS
NATIONAL PARK

Midland

Colorado River

El Paso

Waco

Gladewater

Guadalupe
Peak

Pecos
River

San Angelo

Nacogdoches

AUSTIN

Beaumont

BIG BEND
NATIONAL PARK

Giddings

Houston

Gonzales

Brazos River

Galveston

Rio Grande

San Antonio

Goliad

Matagorda

Laredo

Corpus Christi

Brownsville

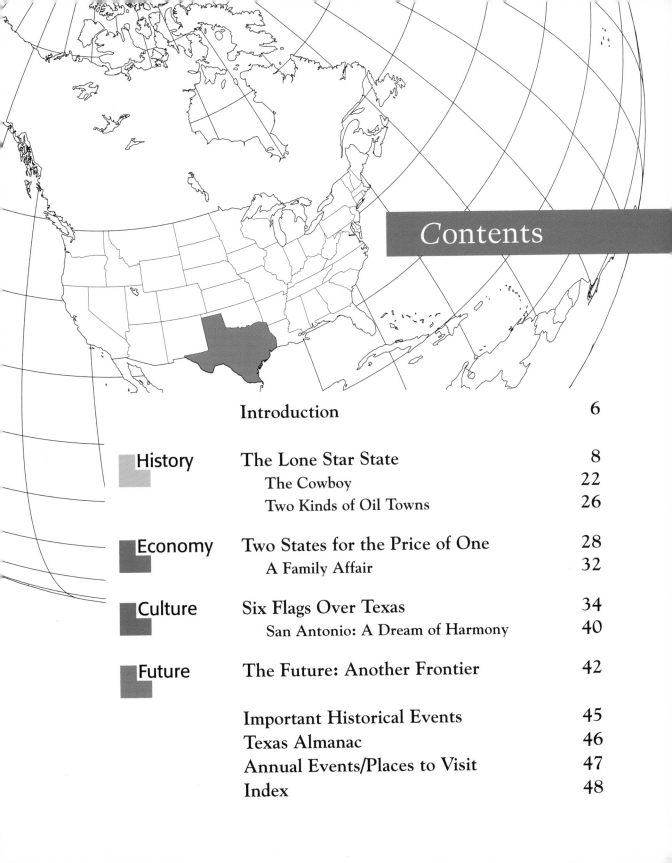

Contents

Introduction

Texas stands alone. That is what the single star on its flag declares. Texans have a spirit of independence. This is a result of the days when Texas was the Lone Star Republic, when it was free from Mexico and not yet a state. Texas has a frontier spirit, too. Cowboys on cattle drives, oil workers, space scientists, business people—Texans are used to making big plans and breaking new ground. And in keeping with its name—a Native American word for "friends"—Texas welcomes all who share its frontier spirit.

Perhaps no state is better symbolized by cowboy boots than Texas. These colorful boots were made in Fort Worth, and each boot has a uniquely Texan theme.

Texas

The Lone Star State

When the Europeans first arrived in the land that would become Texas, the area was sparsely settled. The Native Americans living in the western part were mainly hunters. They lived in camps and hunted with spears and flint-pointed darts.

The Caddo were part of a confederacy of smaller groups of Native Americans that preserved peace and order on a large scale. The Caddo lived in the east in the more fertile regions of the Red River Valley. The Europeans found the land dotted with small farms, each producing enough for its own needs. The Caddo were excellent potters and basketmakers, and they wove their own cloth. Many of the Caddo's religious and political activities were complex, involving ceremony and sacrifice.

In the fall of 1528 a group of Spanish explorers was shipwrecked on the coast of present-day Texas. Eighty men survived the wreck only to be taken prisoner by Native Americans. A harsh winter set in,

Big Bend National Park was once the home of dinosaurs and the Big Bend Pterodactyl, a prehistoric birdlike creature with a wingspan of 51 feet.

above. Francisco Vásquez de Coronado recruited Native Americans to guide his party in the search for gold.

below. During the first one hundred years of Texas' settlement, missions dotted the vast landscape.

and many Native Americans and Spanish died. Only 15 of the Spanish men survived. In time they escaped from their captors and headed toward Spanish Mexico. Only four men—including Álvar Núñez Cabeza de Vaca and Estevanico, who was an African—reached Mexico. These men told stories of golden cities and great wealth, and for many years people believed them. Estevanico would later lead an expedition to search for the golden cities. Cabeza de Vaca's account of his travels includes the earliest written descriptions of this region.

Many more Spanish explorers followed. They wanted to find the fabled golden cities known as the Seven Cities of Cíbola. In 1541 Francisco Vásquez de Coronado set out to explore the area north of the Rio Grande to search for gold. His expedition traveled all the way to present-day Kansas before giving up and returning to Mexico a year later.

In 1682 Spanish Catholic missionaries established Ysleta, the first European settlement in Texas. Other settlements were built nearby in the area of what is now El Paso.

But the Spanish were not the only Europeans who were interested in this great section of the Southwest. In 1685 René-Robert Cavelier, Sieur de La Salle, started a colony near Matagorda Bay that he named Fort Saint Louis. Two years later La Salle was killed by one of his own men. The others in the group died soon after. Sickness took some of them; others were killed by Native Americans who were trying to protect their land. Native Americans then destroyed Fort Saint Louis.

The Spanish continued to send explorers and missionaries into the area. They built missions all over the central, eastern, and southwestern areas of what is now Texas. The settlers built forts to protect the missions from Native Americans. A Spanish government was set up. The Spanish were motivated by the fact that the French were still interested in the area. Although the Spanish redoubled their efforts to settle the area, they were not glad to stay. The Native Americans were still hostile, and the Spanish still had not found any gold. By 1793, after more than one hundred years of missions and explorations, there were still only seven thousand European settlers in Texas.

In 1803 the United States bought the Louisiana Territory from France for $15 million. The United States claimed that the territory included land as far south and west as the Rio Grande. The territory would have included all of what would become Texas. An 1819 treaty, however, designated the Sabine and Red rivers as the accepted boundaries. Texas still belonged to Spain. Later that year Moses Austin visited San Antonio and secured permission to settle Americans in Texas.

In 1821 Mexico won its independence from Spain, and Texas became part of the Empire of Mexico. During this period the population of Texas was about seven thousand. Goliad, Nacogdoches, and San Antonio were the only towns of any size. Newly independent Mexico gave Stephen F. Austin the grant his father sought before he died. Three hundred families would be allowed to settle on two hundred thousand acres of land in Texas. Mexico hoped that the Austin grant would attract and settle new colonists from the United States. In 1823 three hundred families were settled on the Austin grant along the lower Brazos and Colorado rivers. Colonists were drawn by the offer of fertile and inexpensive land. Besides Stephen Austin, some 15 others were also granted land for settlers in the 1820s. In time there were more colonists than Mexicans in Texas.

Friction soon developed between the colonists in Texas—Texans—and the Mexican government. Differences in culture, language, and religion were the main problems. The Texans felt a stronger relationship with the United States than with Mexico. Some Texans hoped that the border of the United States would be extended to include Texas.

In 1830 the Mexican government prohibited further immigration from the United States to Texas. This angered the Texans, who were already displeased about their lack of representation in the Mexican legislature. In 1833 Stephen Austin went to Mexico

In the 1820s Stephen F. Austin founded English-speaking settlements in Texas. The state's capital, Austin, was named in his honor.

City with a list of complaints from the Texans. He succeeded in having the ban on immigration lifted but failed to win a separation of Texas from Mexico. On his way back to Texas, Austin was arrested and held for several months for writing a letter recommending that Texas set up its own government.

In October 1835 war broke out between the Texans and the Mexican government. The Mexican Army was led by General Antonio López de Santa Anna. The Texans forced the retreat of the Mexican cavalry at Gonzales. Later that year, after six weeks of battle, Stephen Austin captured San Antonio. A temporary government was set up with Sam Houston named as commander in chief of the Texas armies. A declaration of independence was made on March 2, 1836, at Washington-on-the-Brazos. A constitution, based closely on that of the United States, was adopted for the new Republic of Texas. Just three days later, Mexican troops captured the Alamo. The siege lasted

above. In 1832 President Andrew Jackson sent Sam Houston to Texas to negotiate treaties with Native Americans. Houston established a home there and soon became one of the Texans' main leaders.

below. The Alamo was the site of a famous battle in which a group of Texas rebels were defeated.

Sam Houston, lying wounded after the Battle of San Jacinto, accepts General Santa Anna's surrender. Santa Anna stands in the center of the picture in white breeches.

José Antonio Navarro was one of the signers of the Texas Declaration of Independence, and he was the only native Mexican at the state's 1845 constitutional convention.

two weeks—183 men died under the command of W. B. Travis. A few days after the Alamo battle, outnumbered Texans were captured and forced to surrender near the San Antonio River. Three hundred and forty-two rebels were marched to the town of Goliad and executed under the orders of General Santa Anna. On April 21, 1836, General Sam Houston's army assaulted Santa Anna's troops near the San Jacinto River during the siesta hour. Santa Anna was captured, and Mexico soon after signed treaties recognizing the independence of Texas.

Sam Houston was elected the first President of Texas. His first act was to try to get the United States to annex the republic. President Andrew Jackson and Congress feared a war with Mexico, however. There was also the question of slavery, which Texas approved of but Northern states opposed. Annexation was finally approved in 1845, but those ten years were very difficult for the "Lone Star Republic." The Texas Rangers, a group of armed lawmen, were formed to provide protection against raids by Native Americans and Mexican outlaws. Also, there was very little money available, and attempts to gain loans from foreign countries failed. Texas did gain a lot of settlers, though. In the decade after independence, the population of Texas climbed from about 50,000 to over 125,000. On December 29, 1845, the United States Congress accepted Texas as the twenty-eighth state.

The Texas Rangers were organized in 1835. Today they are no longer responsible for protecting the frontier, but Rangers still patrol remote areas on horseback and function as special police officers for the state.

After Texas became a state, Mexico and the United States went to war. The leaders of Mexico had not accepted the independence of Texas and had said they would fight to keep it. The war started because of a border dispute. The United States claimed that the border was on the Rio Grande, while the Mexican government claimed it was at the Nueces River.

After two years of fighting, General Winfield Scott's troops captured Mexico City. In the Treaty of Guadalupe Hidalgo, Mexico gave up its claim to Texas and agreed to the Rio Grande as the border. Mexico also gave the United States a large territory that would become the states of California, Utah, New Mexico, Nevada, and Arizona, as well as parts of Colorado and Wyoming. The United States paid Mexico $15 million for this land.

The new state of Texas and the new territory gained in the war with Mexico became caught up in the debate over slavery. Would Texas and the new states created from this land allow slavery? Eventually the debate over slavery led to the Civil War. In 1861 Texas withdrew from the Union and joined the Confederate States of America. About one third of the state's population was against leaving the Union. Governor Sam Houston was strongly opposed to the decision and was removed from office. Still, more than fifty thousand Texans fought on the Confederate side of the war.

Most of the fighting in Texas took place along the coast of the Gulf of Mexico. Union forces tried to invade Texas at several places, including Galveston, Sabine Pass, Brownsville, and the Red River. Each time they were turned back by the Texans. The last battle of the war took place in May 1865 at Palmito Ranch near Brownsville. The soldiers hadn't heard that General Lee had already surrendered at Appomattox a month earlier.

The time after the Civil War—Reconstruction— was a difficult time in the United States. Texas was under military rule for a short time immediately after the war. After the federal government appointed two governors to the state, one Republican governor was elected to office. Republicans were elected in many states throughout the South, supported by a majority of African American voters. The Republicans changed laws that had been unfair to African Americans. Republicans also raised taxes to promote public improvements and economic development. But higher taxes and equality with former slaves angered some

Southerners. To stop African American support for the Republicans, many Southerners resorted to force through the Ku Klux Klan and other organizations. Racial violence occurred throughout the Southern states. On March 30, 1870, Texas was readmitted to the Union. By 1875 all but three Southern states—South Carolina, Louisiana, and Florida—were back in the hands of Southern Democrats.

After the Civil War, many Texans returned to cattle ranching. Cattle roamed the "open range," a vast, fenceless area extending from the Texas Panhandle north to Canada. These were the golden days of the cowboy. Cattle drives began from Texas to the railroad centers in Kansas and Missouri. In western Texas, Native Americans still fought to keep their lands. By 1875

Texas longhorns were rugged enough to survive the harsh conditions of the cattle drive.

During the 1880s railroads began to cross the cattle land of Texas.

Bluebonnets grow on the prairie in some parts of Texas.

many Native Americans had been forced onto a reservation in present-day Oklahoma.

Soon the open range started to close. Towns were established, more railroads were built, and homesteaders bought up the land. Farmers, armed with barbed wire, began sectioning off the open range and planting wheat on the land. By the end of the nineteenth century, after only twenty years, the days of the great cattle drives were over. By this time the population of Texas had grown to more than three million.

Then, in 1901, oil was discovered. The Spindletop oil field near Beaumont gushed more than eighty thousand barrels of oil into the air. The oil boom was on. With the oil came new refineries and big manufacturing plants. The harbors along the coast were now filled with ships ready to take oil anywhere in the world. By

1920 many workers had moved from the rural areas of Texas to work in the oil fields and in the fast-growing cities.

The Great Depression of the 1930s caused millions of people in Texas and across the country to be unemployed. The United States' economy was at a standstill. In Texas, however, the oil industry helped lessen the hardship somewhat. Oil drilling and the manufacture of petroleum products continued.

Also during the 1930s, a severe drought had dried up much of the Great Plains, including Texas. Part of the problem was caused by years of overgrazing and poor farming methods. A series of destructive wind storms easily blew the loose soil away. About fifty million acres of farmland were destroyed in Texas and the Great Plains, known as the "Dust Bowl" states.

The United States entered World War II in 1941. Many people went to work in manufacturing plants

By 1920 oil fields with derricks like the one in the photograph had sprung up all over Texas.

President John F. Kennedy and Jacqueline Kennedy were in Dallas on the day the President was assassinated.

providing war materials. Thousands of people living in ravaged farm areas left the farms to find factory jobs in the cities. People continued to flood into urban areas throughout the decade as industrial expansion continued.

One of the most tragic moments of American history happened in Dallas in 1963. President John F. Kennedy was killed as the car he was riding in passed the Texas School Book Depository. The man accused of shooting him, Lee Harvey Oswald, was himself shot two days later. Lyndon B. Johnson, Kennedy's Vice President, took office as the nation's thirty-sixth President. Johnson, a Texan, was elected to a full term in 1964. That same year President Johnson signed the Civil Rights Act, which made racial discrimination illegal.

In 1962 the National Aeronautics and Space Administration (NASA) built the Manned Spacecraft

Center in Houston. Seven years later Houston scientists and engineers, along with the rest of NASA, put the first astronaut on the moon. The center was renamed the Lyndon B. Johnson Space Center in 1973.

The mid-1980s were a difficult time in Texas. The price of oil and natural gas declined sharply. Many people in the energy industry lost their jobs. Fortunately, many jobs had been created in other industries. These jobs were in health care, computer software, electronics, and aerospace.

Also during the 1980s, women were elected to the highest levels in several Texas cities, including Houston, Dallas, San Antonio, Corpus Christi, and El Paso. In 1990 Ann Richards was elected governor of Texas, becoming only the second woman to hold that office. George W. Bush, Jr., the former President's son, was elected governor in 1994.

Texas now has a larger population than any other state except California. The small farms belonging to the Caddo are gone. So are most of the big cattle ranches. Walking the streets of any of the urban landscapes in Texas, you may still see cowboys and cowboy hats. But Texas stands squarely in the modern world.

Houston is the largest city in Texas. Between 1970 and 1980, a number of corporations opened offices in the city, which resulted in the construction of numerous modern skyscrapers.

The Cowboy

Before there was Texas, there were cowboys. Before there were cowboys, there were *vaqueros*.

Large numbers of American settlers began coming to Texas during the 1820s. Many settlers were impressed with the way the local people, called *vaqueros*, herded cattle. Some even learned the methods of the vaqueros and started using the same kinds of tools. These were the first cowboys. When Texas declared its independence from Mexico in 1836, many of the vaqueros stayed in Texas. They wanted to be Texans, not Mexicans. And in Texas they would be called cowboys, not vaqueros.

The cowboy's life was hard and dangerous. Cowboys had to work outside in all kinds of weather. Out on the open range, it was sometimes hard to get food and water. Still, many Easterners headed west in search of this rougher, more adventurous, and more independent way of life.

After the Civil War, many African Americans left plantations in the South and headed west to become cowboys.

Rodeos were a form of competition and entertainment for cowboys in the late 1800s. Today, cowboys and cowgirls compete in many rodeo events.

Some of the African Americans who had been slaves on ranches in Texas also became cowboys. For the most part, these former slaves were treated just like everybody else on the open range.

In 1865 cowboys began moving large numbers of cattle from Texas northward. A typical cattle drive would employ eight to ten men pushing a

Almost every part of Texas has cattle ranches.

The name for a Mexican cowboy, *vaquero, comes from the Spanish word for cow,* vaca.

Many African Americans moved to the West after the Civil War. About one fourth of all cowboys were African Americans.

herd of two thousand head of longhorn steer. Their job was to get the cattle to one of the cow towns in Kansas. The most famous trail was the Chisolm. It ran from southern Texas through Oklahoma Territory to Ellsworth and Abilene, Kansas. From there the herd was shipped by train to eastern cities. The great trail drives lasted only until the early 1880s. The invention of barbed wire made the drives difficult. And the building of railroads across the West made them unnecessary.

done in the 1800s. It's a tradition. And although most cowboys today are men, there are some women working the roundup. The cowboy lives on—on the plains of West Texas, at least. As long as there are cattle, there will be cowboys.

Rodeos are events that allow men and women to display their roping and horse-riding skills. The events developed out of the everyday ranching activities of cowboys.

There are still some cowboys in Texas. They still know how to rope and ride, but many drive pick-up trucks and use machines to make their work easier. Some cowboys even use heli-copters. A few cowboys prefer to do the roundup just about the way it was

Two Kinds of Oil Towns

Everybody knows about Texas oil and Texas oil millionaires. The oil has been there for millions of years, but there weren't any oil millionaires until about one hundred years ago. Before that time, people didn't need oil, so nobody bothered to look for it. When people in Texas started looking for oil, they often found it right under their feet. The discovery of oil is an important part of the history of many small Texas towns. But oil wasn't what gave most of these towns their start.

After the Civil War, many new railroads were built west of the Mississippi River. With the railroads came brand-new towns. Railroads were very important to small farming communities. If a railroad didn't pass close to a town, the town might have to get closer to the railroad. In 1872 most of the people in the East Texas community of St. Claire moved a few miles away to be closer to a new railroad. They called their new town Gladewater.

In 1931 the people of Gladewater learned that their town was sitting on top of an oil field. The land they had been living on and farming for years was suddenly very valuable. New

In the 1930s one block of downtown Kilgore was nicknamed "the world's richest acre." It had one of the densest concentrations of oil wells in the world.

people rushed in, hoping to get rich. Almost overnight, the population went from five hundred to one thousand. Pretty soon, ten thousand people were living and working in Gladewater. When it got harder to find land with oil under it, people stopped coming. Then, a lot of the fortune-seekers moved on. The boom was over. Life in Gladewater returned to normal—only now some people were rich.

Gladewater wasn't the first boom-town. And it wasn't the only one. Pretty much the same thing happened in places like Kermit and Ranger. Today people still get rich when they find oil, but small towns don't become boomtowns.

About 200 miles southwest of Gladewater is Giddings, Texas. Giddings was founded by a group of German farmers who had come to the United States in 1855 in search of religious freedom. Their first community was about six miles away from the current location of Giddings. When a new railroad was built in 1871, the German settlers moved to be closer to it. And, without knowing it, they built their railroad town on top of oil.

So many people flocked to boomtowns that there were not enough houses for all of them. Instead people lived temporarily in shacks and tents.

Today there are new oil wells in Giddings, but it's still the same small town it always was. The people of Giddings may have more money than their parents and grandparents had, but they share the same faith and the same values. They still live pretty much the way they did before. In Texas, there's plenty of room for different kinds of oil towns and different kinds of oil millionaires.

Two States for the Price of One

If you took a map of Texas and drew a line from the top of the state to the bottom, just west of Dallas, you'd be dividing it into two very different areas. On the eastern side of the line, you'd find most of the big industrial cities. You'd also find cotton and rice farms, pecan groves, and forests. On the western side, you'd find cotton, too. But this is cattle, oil, and wheat country, for the most part.

The dividing line is a natural one. To the east, there's water. And water means rich farmland. Water is also necessary for factories and cities. To the west, there's not much water, but there are rich mineral resources and vast grasslands for cattle grazing.

Most people probably think only of oil and cattle when they think of Texas. After all, Texas ranks first in oil-refining capacity. The Gulf Coast area is the center of the petrochemical industry, producing most of the petrochemicals in the United States. Texas also leads the nation in livestock. The state has large areas of grassland, and the winters are mild enough for cattle to

Texas produces about one quarter of the nation's oil. Most of the oil fields are in the west-central part of the state.

Cotton was first grown in Texas in the 1830s. Today it grows in Texas' coastal region, the northern and central prairie regions, and the Rio Grande Valley.

graze all year long. Texas also raises more sheep than any other state.

Eighty percent of the jobs in Texas are in service industries. Most of these jobs are in health, business, and retail services. What's more, Texas is one of the leading manufacturing states in the country. In fact, it is the chief manufacturing state in the South. Most of the state's manufacturing is linked to petroleum. The biggest industry is oil refining. In addition to fuels and lubricants for cars, planes, and factory equipment, oil refining creates petrochemicals. Thousands of products are made from petrochemicals, including plastics, medicines, insecticides, and paints.

Many of the manufacturing jobs in Texas involve electronics, computers, and industrial machinery. The "Silicon Hills" area around Austin is home to about 450 high-tech companies, providing 55,000 jobs. But food processing also contributes a great deal to the manufacturing industry. This includes meat packing, preparation of grains for flour, and soft drinks.

Products made in Texas are in demand all over the world. In fact, Texas is the second-leading export state. Foreign trade will continue to grow, due to the North American Free Trade Agreement (NAFTA). This agreement makes it easier for companies in the United States, Mexico, and Canada to buy and sell products in each other's countries. Even before NAFTA went into effect, about one third of the products exported from Texas went to Mexico. Jobs are also being created in Texas to help handle the increased flow of goods across the border between the United States and Mexico.

Another rising industry in Texas is construction. Texas' population is expanding quickly. That means more homes need to be built. Companies that produce building materials such as lumber, furniture, fixtures, and stone, clay, and glass masonry are growing rapidly.

The importance of mining—including drilling for oil and natural gas—declined in the 1980s. Oil and gas production now accounts for about 12 percent of the Texas economy. This is about half the production total of 1981. Still, Texas leads the states in mineral and natural gas production. Texas produces about one third of all the natural gas that comes out of the United States every year. Some of the other important minerals found in Texas include sulfur, salt, graphite, magnesium, and many kinds of clay.

Texas is a leading agricultural state, too. The most important crop raised in Texas is cotton, followed by grain sorghum. But there's a lot of wheat and rice grown in the state, too.

The way Texans have made their money has changed. But there's no denying that their economy remains strong. From oil gushers to computer chips, Texans have demonstrated the ability to ride the changing times.

As new residents and businesses move to Texas, the construction industry must keep up with the increase in population.

31

A Family Affair

Burritos, tamales, tacos, refried beans. Even if you've never been to Texas, you may have sampled these Mexican dishes. If you live there, you know that they are a distinctive part of Texas cooking.

In Mercedes, Texas, H & H Foods is a well-known producer of Mexican-style foods and packaged meats. It's not a huge company by national stan-

Ruben Hinojosa is the president of H & H Foods.

dards. But it is the second largest Hispanic-owned food company in the United States—and an outstanding minority enterprise, Texas style!

In 1910 the company's founder Salvador Hinojosa left Mexico with his widowed mother and several siblings. A revolution was just beginning in Mexico. Life north of the Rio Grande in Texas looked safer to the Hinojosas.

By 1947 Salvador and his cousin Atanacio were able to buy a very small meat packing plant in South Texas. The company started out with just three employees. Salvador worked hard. Three years later, H & H—Hinojosa and Hinojosa—had 15 employees.

Atanacio left the business, but Salvador and his family continued. Salvador's wife Marina put her energies into raising their ten children. But the Hinojosas didn't draw a hard line between family and business. At one time, seven of Salvador and Marina's children worked in the company.

Over forty years later, H & H Foods is still a family affair. Four of Salvador's sons run the business. Four grandsons are spurring the growth as their fathers did before them. And the company continues to thrive. During the 1980s,

Employees at H & H Foods package meat.

it won a national award as Outstanding Minority Enterprise, presented in the White House by President Ronald Reagan. By 1994 it employed over three hundred people. Plans are in the works to expand the business. The company is building a new manufacturing plant, which will create 75 to 100 new jobs.

The Hinojosa's family feelings extend to their workers. Ruben Hinojosa, company president, describes his family as one "that believes in taking care of their employees." This means offering them a chance to own shares in H & H. Owning shares helps motivate employees to keep the quality of their prod-

ucts high. H & H Foods prides itself on being bicultural and bilingual—all workers speak English and Spanish.

What does Ruben Hinojosa see as the most important ingredients in his family's success? The "Hinojosa competitiveness" passed down by his parents is one thing. His mother, he says, made sure her ten children were well educated, too. He advises students to "realize that education is the key that opens doors of opportunity. I urge them to dream and be whatever they wish to be. . . . It will be easier to achieve this goal by having an education."

All in all, the H & H story is a typical American success story.

Six Flags Over Texas

Six flags have flown over the land we now call Texas. Their colors are still woven into the fabric of Texas life.

The first flag was the one the Spanish set down on the beach when their boats landed on the shore. Spain came into the culture of the native peoples in Texas as they did in Mexico. In both places the cultures mixed and blended. Today, the strongest evidence of both cultures can be seen in the Mexican American way of life. The Spanish language, the fiestas, the respect for family and religion and the land—these were all part of Texas long before Texas was a part of the United States.

Today, when schools all over the country are struggling with the problems of Spanish-speaking students in an English-speaking system, it is important to remember that Texas once had a school system in which only Spanish was spoken. That was one of the reasons that American settlers rebelled against Mexican rule.

The flags of Spain, France, and Mexico have all flown over Texas. The many episodes of Texas history have helped shape its culture.

It is inaccurate to think of the Mexican culture in Texas as a foreign influence. It is as much a part of Texas as rodeos and oil wells are. To experience the Mexican influence on Texas life, you need only visit many of the towns along the border. In Laredo, for example, mariachis are often heard serenading visitors. A mariachi band is a small group of Mexican singers. They dress in traditional Mexican costumes and sing and play traditional songs. Many towns hold Mexican fiestas, which celebrate Mexican culture with food, lively music, and bright original costumes. Mexican art and crafts, such as pottery, masks, and handweaving, are on display in museums throughout Texas.

Mexican culture has certainly influenced the variety of food in Texas. Menu items such as burritos, tacos, chile peppers, and chimichangas are distinctly Mexican in origin and in flavor. Be careful; some of these are spicy hot!

Many former activities distinctly thought of as belonging to Texas were brought north from Mexico. This is a part of Mexican culture not often on display in Texas, but it still lives in legends. The Mexican *vaqueros* taught the American cowboys the essential techniques of branding, roundups, and roping.

The culture of Hispanic peoples in Texas began at the time of the Spanish missions over three hundred years ago.

Much of the clothing and tools that cowboys used in those days were originally Mexican, also.

The flag of France flew over Texas between the times of the Spanish and Mexican flags, but it wasn't there long. There is not much in Texas today to remind us that France had ever established a colony in East Texas. Three flags have been counted now. And then there was the fourth—the flag of the Republic of Texas.

You might think that flag was unimportant, too. After all, Texas is Texas, whether it's a country or a state. But there's a certain pride in being a Texan that is as strong as the pride in being an American.

The Republic of Texas came about when colonists in Texas broke away from Mexico. They declared their independence from the Mexican government in much the same way that the original 13 American colonies declared their independence from England. A number of historic sites still exist that tell the story of the Texas Revolution. The first skirmish of the Revolution took place in Gonzales only ten years after it was settled. The people of Goliad have preserved the site of the famous "Goliad Massacre," a major incident in the Revolution. The Alamo, known as the "Cradle of Texas Liberty," is probably the best-remembered battle site of the Texas Revolution.

Rodeo is a Texas tradition. Today there are all-female rodeos where women compete in events like bull riding and bareback bronc riding.

Millions of people attend the Texas State Fair in Dallas every October.

These colorful flowers are found in Big Bend National Park. Nature lovers have plenty of places to explore in Texas.

The fifth flag is that of the Confederacy. Texas was one of the states that withdrew from the Union and joined the Confederacy during the Civil War. This flag is important because it means that Texas, more than the other states of the Southwest, can be called a Southern state. There are parts of Texas that have much more in common with Alabama and Missouri than with Arizona and New Mexico. There were once plantations in East Texas. And there were slaves. Texas often votes in national elections the way that the southern states vote. There are shared values and traditions.

The sixth flag over Texas is the flag of the United States of America. Texas joined the Union as the twenty-eighth state on December 29, 1845.

The six flags represent the history of Texas from the days of European exploration. Although the Native Americans did not own a flag or have a purpose for one, their culture is represented also. The town of Quanah is named for the great chief of the Comanche. Nearby are the famous Medicine Mounds. The Comanche believed the mounds were the dwelling place of powerful and peaceful spirits.

Texas culture is a blend of all these influences. The six flags show the respect that Texans have for those who shaped their history.

People enjoy fishing in Texas' many creeks, lakes, rivers, and coastal areas.

Native American ceremonies are very much a part of Texas culture. Ceremonies usually include dances that tell a story. Costumes such as the one shown here help to present the story.

San Antonio: A Dream of Harmony

San Antonio is a city of differences. Within its boundaries two cultures live side by side—but not always together.

Together, Mexican Americans and people who came to the United States from Central America and South America make up the largest minority group in Texas. But in San Antonio, they are not a minority. They are a majority. For many years, they lived in areas called *barrios*. The people who lived in the barrios mostly kept to themselves. They didn't have much to do with the city government or the business community.

Life in the barrios was difficult. After rains fell, it was not unusual for these low-lying parts of the city to flood. There were other things that made life in the barrios difficult, including poor schools, poverty, and

The COPS convention drew a large number of participants.

San Antonio's River Walk is lined with palm trees and tropical plants. Its shops, restaurants, and pleasant atmosphere make it a popular leisure-time spot.

poor housing. A lot of other problems came with those conditions. Crime increased. More and more marriages ended in divorce. People felt hopeless. Many people who could afford to move away did just that.

Then a group of people from the barrios got together and decided that things had to change. Sonia Hernandez and Beatrice Cortez helped form a group called COPS—Communities Organized for Public Service. They registered people in the barrios so that they could vote. They helped elect a Mexican American, Henry Cisneros, as mayor of the city. They got the local government to work on the flooding, education, and housing.

Today life is easier for the people who live in the barrios. The barrios are no longer set apart from the rest of San Antonio. Their values—including a deep respect for the family and the neighborhood—have had a positive influence on the city. Now the business community and the people of the barrios work together for the good of the entire community.

The Mexican American culture makes San Antonio stand out from other United States cities. That, along with pleasant weather and attractions, such as the River Walk and the Alamo, help bring conventions and tourists to town. San Antonio has gained a lot from the Mexican American community.

The Future: Another Frontier

Texas has always been a frontier state. The people enjoy the challenge of pushing forward into new places where no one has ever been. They like breaking new ground. That may be why Texas, for all its roots in the past, looks with eagerness to the future. For the people of this sprawling state, the future is just one more frontier.

Texas' universities are doing research in space medicine. Several corporations design and test space equipment. And of course, there is the Lyndon B. Johnson Space Center, a part of the National Aeronautics and Space Administration (NASA). Texas is helping the country push farther into space.

Many national corporations are choosing the large cities of Texas for their homes. In Dallas and Houston, glass and steel office buildings reach high into the sky. Along the Mexican border, towns are taking on a new, busier look as trade activity increases.

Tens of thousands of people move to Texas every year from other parts of the country. They are drawn

As the main producer of the country's oil, Texas has also become a major producer of the chemicals and other products that use oil as a raw material.

Texans support higher education in their state. The University of Texas offers programs in science, medicine, the arts, law, business, humanities, technology, and other fields.

by the feeling that Texas is "where it's happening." Texas is the future.

But Texas has important problems to solve in the years to come, too. The most important is helping all its people share in the wealth of the land. Texas ranks high among all the states in total personal income. But it ranks much lower in income per person. In other words, there are quite a few people in Texas who have a lot of money. But there are many, many more who have very little. When Texas meets this challenge, it will have crossed perhaps its most important frontier.

Important Historical Events

1519 Alonso Álvarez de Piñeda explores the coast of Texas.

1528 Álvar Núñez Cabeza de Vaca and three others explore parts of the region.

1541 Francisco Vásquez de Coronado passes through West Texas.

1682 Spanish missionaries build the first missions in Texas, near what is today El Paso.

1685 René-Robert Cavelier, Sieur de La Salle, founds Fort Saint Louis.

1690 The Franciscans establish the first mission in East Texas.

1691 Texas becomes a Spanish dominion.

1821 Stephen F. Austin founds American settlements.

1830 Mexico stops Americans from settling in Texas.

1835 The first battle of the Texas Revolution takes place.

1836 Texas declares its independence. The Alamo falls to General Santa Anna. General Sam Houston captures Santa Anna at the battle of San Jacinto. Texas becomes an independent republic.

1845 Texas becomes the 28th state on December 29.

1846 War between Mexico and the United States begins.

1861 Texas secedes from the Union.

1865 The last Civil War battle is fought near Brownsville.

1866 The first oil well in Texas is drilled in Nacogdoches.

1870 Texas is readmitted to the Union.

1876 The present state constitution is adopted.

1881 The Southern Pacific Railroad links Texas with California.

1901 The Spindletop oil field produces the first gusher in North America.

1914 The Houston Ship Channel is opened.

1925 Miriam A. Ferguson becomes the first woman governor of Texas and the second woman governor in the United States.

1952 Dwight D. Eisenhower, born in 1890 in Denison, is elected the 34th president of the United States.

1953 Congress restores Texas tidelands to the state.

1963 President John F. Kennedy is assassinated in Dallas. Vice President Lyndon B. Johnson, born in 1908 near Stonewall, becomes President.

1964 The Manned Spacecraft Center in the Houston area becomes the headquarters of United States astronauts.

1969 Amistad (Friendship) Dam, on the Rio Grande, is completed—to serve both the United States and Mexico.

1976 Texas Congresswoman Barbara Jordan becomes the first African American to deliver the keynote address at the Democratic National Convention.

1978 William P. Clements becomes the first Republican to be elected governor since 1869.

1990 Ann Richards becomes the second woman governor of Texas.

1994 George W. Bush, the former President's son, is elected governor.

The state flag of Texas was adopted in 1839. The lone star represents the state's nickname "The Lone Star State." The red symbolizes courage, the white stands for purity, and the blue represents loyalty.

Texas Almanac

Nickname. The Lone Star State

Capital. Austin

State Bird. Mockingbird

State Flower. Bluebonnet

State Tree. Pecan

State Motto. Friendship

State Song. "Texas, Our Texas"

State Abbreviations. Tex. (traditional); TX (postal)

Statehood. December 29, 1845, the 28th state

Government. Congress: U.S. senators, 2; U.S. representatives, 30. State Legislature: senators, 31; representatives, 150. Counties: 254

Area. 266,874 sq mi (691,201 sq km), 2nd in size among the states

Greatest Distances. north/south, 737 mi (1,186 km); east/west, 774 mi (1,245 km). Coastline: 367 mi (591 km)

Elevation. Highest: Guadalupe Peak, 8,751 ft (2,667 m). Lowest: sea level, along the Gulf of Mexico

Population. 1990 Census: 17,059,805 (20% increase over 1980), 2nd among the states; Density: 64 persons per sq mi (25 persons per sq km). Distribution: 80% urban, 20% rural. 1980 Census: 14,227,574

Economy. *Agriculture:* beef cattle, cotton. *Fishing:* shrimp, crabs. *Manufacturing:* lumber products, chemicals, food products, electrical equipment, petroleum products, machinery, transportation equipment. *Mining:* petroleum, natural gas

State Seal

State Flower: Bluebonnet

State Bird: Mockingbird

Annual Events

★ Houston Livestock Show and Rodeo Exposition (February-March)

★ Texas Independence Day (March)

★ Jefferson Historical Pilgrimage in Jefferson (April-May)

★ Watermelon Thump in Luling (June)

★ Aqua Festival in Austin (August)

★ East Texas Yamboree in Gilmer (October)

★ Texas State Fair in Dallas (October)

★ Festival of Lights in San Antonio (December)

Places to Visit

★ The Alamo in San Antonio

★ Big Bend National Park

★ Lyndon B. Johnson Space Center in Houston

★ McDonald Observatory at Mt. Locke, near Fort Davis

★ Mission San Jose in San Antonio

★ Moody Gardens in Galveston

★ Padre Island National Seashore

★ San Jacinto Monument in Houston

★ Texas Ranger Museum in Waco

★ Texas State Aquarium in Corpus Christi

Index